MIRACLES OF ST. PHILARET
METROPOLITAN OF MOSCOW

Especially remarkable instances of the action of Divine Grace through Metropolitan Philaret of Moscow during his lifetime.

Taken from "Miracles of Metropolitan Philaret of Moscow," The Society of Enthusiasts of Orthodox Culture, Moscow, 1994.

Holy Trinity Monastery Printshop
Jordanville, NY 13361
2003

Printed with the Blessing of
Metropolitan Laurus
of Eastern America and New York

Published by Holy Trinity Monastery, Jordanville,
NY 13361-0036

+

In Memory of
Oleg Selawry

Portrait of Metropolitan Philaret by Archimandrite Cyprian

Preface

St. Philaret, Metropolitan of Moscow: a Godly intercessor for our difficult times.

Nineteenth century Russia witnessed a flowering of outstanding hierarchs of great saintliness and erudition, among whom was St. Philaret, Metropolitan of Moscow. He was one of those very rare persons who combined intellectual brilliance with asceticism and intense spiritual knowledge, yet was available to all who approached him, in many cases working miracles on their behalf.

St. Philaret was born in 1782 in the city of Kolomna. Being the son of a priest, he learned to love the Church at an early age, and at the age of sixteen he entered the seminary, where he excelled in Greek and Ancient Hebrew, and in time became a teacher of those languages in the seminary. When a young man, he showed a great talent in writing poetry, and later taught poetry as well. At the age of twenty-three he was tonsured a monk. His intellectual brilliance soon won him a place in influential circles in the Church and in the Imperial court. He was ordained, and raised to the rank of Archimandrite within a few years, and in 1815 he published his first of what would be many books, the bulk of which were sermons, for which he became renowned; they were simple, direct, yet theologically and spiritually profound.

When he became Metropolitan of Moscow, his beneficial influence could be seen in many aspects of Church life and Russian society in general. He was very prominent in the Russian Bible Society's endeavor to publish a translation of the Bible in Russian. He steadfastly maintained the integrity of the position of the Church when government reforms were attempted after the Crimean War. His students never forgot his greatness as a teacher, and his kindness and attention to them during his term as dean of the St. Petersburg Academy. The catechism which he wrote remains a standard to this day. He was an intellectual, a poet, an adept statesman, a brilliant administrator, a staunch patriot, a concerned archpastor, an inspiring homilist, a wonder-worker, a Saint.

Since his Glorification by the Russian Church Outside Russia in Munich, Germany in May of 2001, there has been an increased interest in the life and works of the Holy Hierarch. His wonderful sermons and speeches have seen an increase in translation into English, for in them is found much wisdom and inspiration for all Orthodox Christians. On November 1-2, 2002, an important symposium was sponsored by Holy Trinity Orthodox Seminary in Jordanville, New York on the theme, "Philaret, Metropolitan of Moscow (1782-1867): Perspectives on the Man, his Works, and his Times," attracting a number of professors, scholars, seminary teachers and students from all over North America and from Russia. Commencing with a talk given by His Eminence, Mark, Archbishop of Berlin and Germany, a series of lectures was given on various themes elucidating the Metropolitan's significant role in Church and Russian history, the result of which has generated renewed interest in the life of this remarkable man, and especially his sanctity.

Along with his many intellectual gifts, St. Philaret was a great ascetic and a man of prayer, a true man of God. The purpose of this small volume is to present the fruits of his love for God and his neighbor - some of his many miracles. It will be seen how he was available to all from prince to peasant, to the sick and the well, the poor and rich, anyone who sincerely asked his prayers and blessing. With a word, the gift of a small icon, in a dream, or in a miraculous appearance, he came to the aid of those in need as befits a true shepherd of his flock. May you be inspired by these wondrous deeds of St. Philaret, and may his love for Christ our Saviour touch your heart! St. Philaret, pray to God for us!

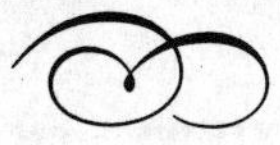

С͠Т. ФИЛАРЕТЪ
МР. МОСКОВСКІЙ

MIRACLES OF ST. PHILARET METROPOLITAN OF MOSCOW

Especially remarkable instances of the action of Divine Grace through Metropolitan Philaret of Moscow during his lifetime.

(1)

Once, M. A. S. was seriously sick with a fever, and when the doctors said that there was no more hope of recovery, his brother A. S., seeking the prayers of the saints, went to his Eminence, Metropolitan Philaret of Moscow, who was preparing to serve the Divine Liturgy on that day. When his request was conveyed, Vladyka ordered that the name of the sick man be written down for commemoration. Returning home, A. S. found his brother completely unconscious, but after a short time his brother opened his eyes and with a very weak voice said, "I believe I will be well." When asked why he was so sure that he would be well, he said, "In my sleep I saw that I was standing in church, and I saw Vladyka going into the altar to the Table of Oblation, where he took out a particle from a prosphora, which he then handed to me with the words: 'Here is a prosphora for your health'." It was then that A. S. told him that he had asked Vladyka for his holy prayers. From that time the sick man began to improve and within a short time he was completely healthy.

(2)

The Moscow merchant V. was stricken with a serious cold and because of this, gangrene formed on his hand. Not seeing any way of treating it, the doctors decided to amputate the hand and scheduled the day for the operation. On the day before this terrifying event, a schismatic [Old Believer] woman came to see the household servants of the merchant. When she asked about the merchant's health, they told her that his hand was decaying more and more, and that they would amputate it on the following day. Hearing this, the schismatic said sarcastically," Why don't you turn to your Metropolitan? You honor him as a saint, don't you?"

But this sarcasm was taken as inspiration, and the wife of the sick man immediately set out with her son to speak to His Eminence, Metropolitan Philaret, and ask his holy prayers for her husband. Hearing her request, Vladyka sent for their parish priest, who came quickly. Having questioned the priest about the sick man, Vladyka directed the priest to commune the sick man with the Holy Mysteries of Christ, and to serve for forty days the Divine Liturgy for his health.

In the evening of that day, the sick man fell into a light sleep, during which he saw Vladyka blessing him. Upon awakening, he told his wife about his dream and asked that he be brought the Holy Gifts, despite the fact that, until this time, regardless of his dangerous situation, he constantly delayed fulfilling this Christian duty. At that time, to his own amazement, he noticed that the illness, which had progressed so rapidly, suddenly ended. On the following day, he received the Holy Mysteries of Christ, and when the doctors arrived at the appointed time for the operation, they were struck by the unusual change in the condition of the patient, for his hand had assumed its natural appearance: it had become white, and there was no need for the operation. V. and his relatives gave thanks to the Lord, who, through the prayers of Vladyka, had performed this amazing healing.

(3)

N. N. related to me the following story about his son: while his son was still a baby, his whole body was covered in sores from tuberculosis. Many doctors tried to treat him, but without success. Finally, someone advised the mother to turn to Metropolitan Philaret, to ask for his holy prayers and blessing. She set out to the Holy Trinity Metochion (Dependency), but Vladyka was not receiving anyone at that time due to his own illness. She earnestly implored Vladyka Philaret's cell attendant to pass on to him her request to give his blessing to the sick baby, even in absentia. When this was conveyed to Vladyka, he sent the mother a small icon of St. Sergius and directed her to pray to him for her son's health.

Having returned home, she placed the icon on the sick child, and after two weeks, all the sores disappeared from his body. At present, her son is already fourteen years old and completely healthy.

(4)

On October 16, 1849, His Eminence Metropolitan Philaret performed the consecration of the church dedicated to the Protection of the Most Holy Theotokos. After Liturgy, he honored the home of the merchant E. with his presence. The four-year-old daughter of the merchant up to this time hardly spoke to anyone, but continually cried in the morning and evening, she herself not understanding why. When she was brought to Vladyka, he blessed her and placed his hand on her head. From that day, she stopped crying and the following morning she freely read the prayer: "O Virgin Theotokos Rejoice" - and began to speak.

(5)

The woman V. was a tutor in a merchant's home, but she was in poor health and experienced great pain in her chest and back, so that frequently she had to leave work. One time, when she was very sick, E., at whose house she worked, saw Metropolitan Philaret in a dream - he was standing in a broad field, holding two blessed breads, one of which he gave to her, saying, "Does V. live with you?" E. answered that V. did not live with her, but only came to tutor her children, and that she is now sick. Then Vladyka gave E. the other blessed bread saying, "Give this to her." After taking the blessed breads and receiving a blessing from Vladyka, E. woke up. Two days later, V. came to her, and when she was asked how she felt, she answered that she started feeling better two days ago.

The day that she started to feel better was the very day that E. saw her dream. From that time she began to recover and has not experienced chest or back pain for twenty years now.

(6)

One priest had a seriously ill daughter. At that time, he was to be awarded a skufia by His Eminence, Metropolitan Philaret. Receiving the award, and a blessing, he mentally asked Vladyka to pray for the health of his daughter. When he returned home, he, with faith, placed the skufia on the head of the sick girl, after which she fell asleep. The next day, she rose from bed, completely healthy.

(7)

A. F. K. became so seriously ill that in spite of medical assistance, the illness was gaining the upper hand. While in this condition, the sick woman saw, in a dream, Metropolitan Philaret, who blessed her and said, "You will be well." Upon wakening, she actually did feel better, and from that time, to the amazement of the doctors, she completely recovered.

(8)

Mr. S. was sick with a fever, and in spite of all the efforts of the doctors to induce him to perspire, they were unsuccessful, and despaired of his recovery. While he was in such a feverish state, he fell asleep, and saw Vladyka, who entered his room with a censer in his hand. Having censed the entire room, he approached the bed and asked, "What is wrong with you?" The sick man answered that he was sick. Vladyka said to him, "Go and buy three sheets of silver leaf, swallow them and you will recover." Upon awakening, the patient sent for the sheets of silver leaf, and following Vladyka's instructions, he swallowed them, and what happened? From the high fever came profuse perspiration, which caused his sickness to vanish completely.

(9)

A. G. G., who respected Vladyka very much, was suffering from throat consumption, which had progressed to such a degree that she could swallow nothing but water. Realizing the danger of her condition, she sincerely desired to partake of the Holy Mysteries of Christ, but the priest, fearing that she was in no condition to swallow the Holy Gifts, delayed in fulfilling her desire. Therefore, having faith in the prayers of Vladyka, she asked her husband to go to him and ask for his holy prayers and blessing, which he did. Having listened to him, Vladyka summoned their parish priest. When he came, Vladyka asked him why he decided not to give the Holy Mysteries to the sick woman. When he explained the reason, Vladyka said to him, "Tomorrow serve Liturgy for the health of the sick woman, and with faith and hope in the mercy of God, give her the Holy Gifts." The next day, by Vladyka's prayers, an unusual miracle happened with the sick woman: she felt relief in her throat, and when the priest, according to Vladyka's order, served the Liturgy and came with the Holy Gifts, to his and all the relatives amazement, she was able easily to partake of the Holy Mysteries of the Body and Blood of Christ.

(10)

For thirty years N. N. was ailing, the result of which was that his character was very hot-tempered. Once, at the end of September 1856, he was more irritable than usual for the course of two weeks. Finally, on October 5, the feast day of the Moscow Hierarchs Peter, Alexis, and Jonah, his sister-in-law saw in a dream that she was going to the Holy Trinity Metochion. She asked that her arrival be announced to Vladyka, who told her to come into one of his rooms. Upon entering, she stopped and saw that Vladyka was leaving the room by an opposite door. Sitting down at a desk, he took a small piece of paper, made the sign of the cross, and began to write. Quickly he wrote one page and then another, and signed his name at the end. On the fourth page was an image of a saint in an epitrachelion. After this he gave her the note and said, "Do not grieve; the Lord will comfort you." Having said this, Vladyka departed into his inner chamber.

Taking the note, she read the following: "Beloved in Christ, brother Zosima! I entrust you this suffering woman who has the misfortune of living with a brother-in-law with a cruel character. Comfort and reassure her, but only so that..." At this point she awoke, not having read more than one and a half pages, and related the dream to her husband and the fact that all of the words read by her in her dream were firmly imprinted in her memory. In the morning, when they gathered for tea, she noticed a drastic change in her brother-in-law. He had become kind and attentive, as if trying to smooth over the past. Seeing this, the sister-in-law could not hold back her tears and had to leave the room, giving thanks to the Lord, Who through the prayers of the righteous had sent her consolation. From that day on, N. N. greatly changed for the better.

In April of 1857, he became very ill and his doctor said that he had only one week to live. He suffered from a high fever and cysts in his mouth, and at his age there was nothing they could do (he was 64 years old). The sister-in-law sent word to Vladyka, asking for his prayers for the sick man. On April 23, Vladyka served the Divine Liturgy in the church at the foundling hospital. He commemorated the sick man, taking a particle from a prosphora, which N. N. then gratefully received from Vladyka. On the following day, N. N. could already sit up and the doctor declared him out of danger, admitting that the Lord healed him when man could not. After this, N. N. was sick for another ten and a half months, but for a cough and some swelling, he felt no discomfort. But in March of 1858, he began to experience shortness of breath and coughing, and the swelling in his legs increased. On Palm Sunday, N. N. partook of Holy Communion. He became more and more weak, and his character became gentler and gentler. Often they would find him in tears, gazing at the icons and making the sign of the cross. On April 16, he received the Holy Mysteries again, as well as Holy Unction, after which he ate no food for a whole day. On April 17, he called his sister-in-law. When she saw how weak he was, she summoned the priest to come and read the "Canon for the Departure of the Soul." When this was done, at the end of the final prayer, N. N. peacefully reposed.

This was the feast day of St. Zosima, the Wonderworker of Solovki, to whom, one and a half years before, Vladyka had entrusted the sister-in-law of the newly-reposed man, so that he could console her. This request the Saint of God completely fulfilled; first, with the change of character of N. N., and secondly, with his Christian death.

(11)

One nun who was in Moscow collecting alms greatly suffered from rheumatism in the cheek. Once, after Liturgy, which Vladyka served in Chudov Monastery, she approached him to receive his blessing, and she dared to put his hand to her ailing cheek, with the hope of receiving relief, and in fact, from that day, the illness completely vanished.

(12)

There was one eight-year-old girl who was feeble and could not walk. Her mother, on hearing that Vladyka would consecrate a church not far from her home, decided to take her to the service. They carried her into church and sat her down on a stool. At the end of the service, when they went to receive a blessing from Vladyka, they carried her in their arms. Vladyka blessed her, and in a short time, with the help of others, she stood and already could walk out of the church herself, and soon walked freely on her own.

(13)

As a result of a cold, N. N. was experiencing angina and could not even swallow water. Therefore, the doctors decided to operate on her the following morning. That night, she fell asleep and saw Vladyka enter her room, approach her, and say, "I came to bless you." Saying this, he blessed her. Having received the blessing, she awoke and felt relief in her throat. When she asked them to give her a cup of tea and drank it freely, the doctors saw that there was no need for the operation, and she fully recovered.

(14)

The daughter of a certain deacon was so seriously ill so that her death was awaited. Therefore, when going to church to serve with Vladyka the next time, he bid farewell to his daughter, thinking he would not see her alive again. Before the beginning of Liturgy, the deacon asked Vladyka to commemorate her in his holy prayers, to which Vladyka replied, "Together we will pray." Asking her name, he took a particle out of the prosphora for her health. When they finished the service, Vladyka blessed the deacon and said, "Do not despair; God is merciful." When he returned home, to his great surprise, he found his daughter out of any danger. From that day, she began to improve and soon she completely healed.

(15)

Once, while going to the Holy Trinity Metochion, N. N. met an unknown woman who was weeping bitterly. When asked the reason for her sorrow, she answered that her husband had severe drinking binges, and when she went to ask Metropolitan Philaret for his holy prayers, they would not let her see him. Feeling sorry for her, N. N. told her that when Vladyka was to go to services, that she should approach him for a blessing and tell Vladyka about her husband, and ask him to pray for him. She was very happy with this advice, and did what she was told. And what happened? Soon her husband was completely delivered from his drunken-ness.

(16)

In 1850, the daughter of a Moscow merchant, E., suffered from serious rheumatism in her entire body and none of the efforts of the doctors could help her. Because of the severe pain, she could not even lie down. If she did sleep briefly, it was while sitting, and leaning on a pillow. She endured this terrible condition for about three weeks. On the night of March 3rd, her mother saw Vladyka in a dream. He came to their home, and after a brief conversation, at her request, he went to bless the sick girl. Approaching her, he blessed her very slowly, as if he was reading a prayer, and with this, the dream ended. As a result of the dream, the mother of the sick girl went to the Holy Trinity Metochion, and giving the name of her daughter, asked Vladyka to remember her in his holy prayers. Returning home, she told her daughter that she had been to see Vladyka, and this made the girl very happy. Within two hours, the sick girl, up to that time in serious condition, unexpectedly felt improvement to the amazement of all those around her, and for the first in three weeks, she lay down and slept soundly for more than twelve hours. Having awakened at 9:00 in the morning, she said that she had seen Vladyka in a dream, and that he had blessed her. When her parents asked her how she felt, she answered that she felt absolutely no pain. As proof, she stood up and read the morning prayers.

On the following day, March 5, having celebrated the Liturgy in the Chudov Monastery, Vladyka sent a prosphora for her health, which she received with great reverence. In spite of eating only fasting food during Great Lent, even against doctor's orders, in a short time, she became significantly stronger.

(17)

While living in the city of Kaliazin, S. suffered greatly for a long time from attacks of demonic possession. Her husband tried all possible means to relieve her suffering, but everything failed to help. Once, in a dream, she heard a voice saying to her, "Go to Moscow, and there you will receive healing from Metropolitan Philaret." When she woke up, she told her husband about her dream. Her husband decided immediately to take her to Moscow. After their arrival, he took her to see Vladyka, and having explained to him her sickness, asked Vladyka to pray for her. Since this was just before Great Lent, Vladyka told her to fast and to prepare to receive Communion at the end of the first week of the Fast. Having served the Divine Liturgy on Saturday, he communed her, along with others, of the Holy Mysteries, at which time she experienced a terrible demonic attack. On the eve of the feast of St. Alexis of Moscow, she went with a relative to the evening services at the Chudov monastery, where Vladyka was serving. At the end of the service she wanted to venerate the holy relics of St. Alexis, but because of powerful attacks, she could not do so. She was taken by her relative to the Holy Trinity Metochion so that she could more easily receive a blessing from Vladyka. When Vladyka returned from the service, she approached him to receive a blessing. He blessed her with these words: "Through the prayers of St. Alexis, I bless you."

Throughout all of Great Lent she attended services at the Holy Trinity Metochion daily, and during this time her attacks, although they continued, became much weaker. In the fourth week, according to Vladyka's directions, she prepared for Communion for a second time, and was communed by him of the Holy Mysteries in the church of the Piatnitsky cemetery. This time her attack was already barely noticeable. When Vladyka served the Divine Liturgy on Holy Saturday in the church at the Holy Trinity Metochion, she freely approached to receive the Holy Mysteries of Christ, and after that, the attacks never returned. Seeing such a miracle, she and her husband went to Vladyka to thank him joyfully for her miraculous healing. Refusing their gratitude, he told them to thank St. Alexis, saying that by his prayers God had granted her healing. From that time on, until her death, she remained completely well.

(18)

One landowner told the following: on his estate was a young woman who was able to speak until she was seventeen years of age. Then, having been frightened, she lost her speech, and despite all the efforts to cure her, remained mute. When she was twenty years old, her parents went with her to the St. Sergius-Holy Trinity Lavra and to the Gethsemane Skete, which had just been built, where Vladyka was staying. At the entrance of the skete, the gatekeeper stopped them, saying that women were not allowed to enter. But they implored him to let them in to see Vladyka, whom they called *"Nabolshim"* [dialect for "the boss"], saying that they had heard that he would give them medicine that would help their daughter. Seeing their determination, the gatekeeper decided to tell Vladyka about them. Vladyka ordered that they be brought to him. Coming before him, they fell at his feet, explained the reason from their visit, and begged him to help their daughter in some way. Having heard their request, Vladyka spoke to the dumb woman with the words, "What is your name?" Her mother hastened to answer for her, saying that her name was Maria. "And I asked *you*," Vladyka said, directing his words to the young woman, and he repeated the question. To the great amazement of her parents, she answered, "Maria." After this, Vladyka said, "Repeat after me the Lord's Prayer, the Our Father." She began to repeat the words after him, but very slowly. After finishing the prayer, Vladyka blessed her and directed her to repeat the prayer again, which she did, this time with complete ease. Seeing such a miracle, the surprised parents fell at the feet of Vladyka and thanked him for the healing of their daughter. Vladyka blessed them and strictly forbade them to talk about this. After that the girl spoke normally.

(19)

In 1857, B. was extremely ill, and at the request of her relatives who saw the hopelessness of her situation, she received the Holy Mysteries and the Anointing of the Sick. After this, B. was completely conscious, and awaiting her approaching death, turned to the portrait of Vladyka that was hanging in her room and mentally asked his holy prayers and blessings. After this she felt some relief, and the next day she sent her daughter to Vladyka to ask for his holy prayers. Vladyka received her daughter, and when she related the request of her mother, he asked the name of the sick woman, and sent her a small icon of St. Sergius. After receiving the icon, the sick woman felt much better and became well, after which she lived for twelve more years.

(20)

In a serious condition from a high fever, N. N. fell asleep, and in a dream he saw Vladyka serving the Vigil with other hierarchs in the church of St. Nicholas the Wonderworker. When during the singing of "Praise ye the name of the Lord," Vladyka was censing the church and passed by him, he bowed down and kissed Vladyka's foot, and after this he awoke. From that day his sickness subsided, and he became well.

(21)

One woman related the following concerning herself: "At one time, having suffered for three months with a sore throat, from which an abscess had formed in my throat, I saw in a dream that Vladyka was coming to the home of my friends and I was hurrying to receive his blessing. Vladyka blessed me and placed his hand on my head. After this I awoke, and felt a great relief, and in less than an hour the abscess burst and I regained my health."

(22)

N. N. became so seriously ill that she was given the Anointing of the Sick and her family awaited her death. At that time, her brother was at the Holy Trinity Metochion, and asked Vladyka, through his secretary, to pray for the sick woman. Vladyka sent her oil and holy water. The next day she absolutely wanted a small icon from Vladyka, so one of her relatives went to the Holy Trinity Metochion. Since Vladyka was not receiving anyone that day because of his own illness, the relative asked Vladyka's secretary to pass on the request of the sick woman. Vladyka sent her a small icon of St. Sergius. Her family placed the icon on her and she immediately fell into a deep sleep, which continued for six hours. When she woke up, she felt much better, and soon was healthy again.

(23)

L. P., who lived in the city of P., was hopelessly sick, and having great faith in the prayers of Vladyka, wanted to receive from him the blessing of a small icon. Her desire was conveyed to her relatives who lived in Moscow, by whose request Vladyka sent her a small image of Our Saviour Not-Made-By-Hands. The sick woman received the icon with tears of joy and told them to place it on her. From that day on she became better and regained her health.

(24)

M. A. was very ill, and even in a state of frenzy. One of his acquaintances, seeing him in such a pitiful condition, went to Vladyka, and telling him the name of the sick man, asked him to pray for him. Amazingly, from that day M. A. felt some relief and within a short time he was completely healed.

(25)

One merchant traveled to Kiev because of a promise he had made. On the return trip, near Tula, robbers accosted him, demanding all of his money. Seeing his unwillingness to hand it over, they threatened him with death. At that terrifying moment, there suddenly resounded from afar the sound of an approaching carriage. Becoming afraid, the robbers ran into the forest. Seeing himself out of danger he moved closer to the road, and approaching the carriage he saw in it the Metropolitan, with whom he was entirely unacquainted, who gave him his blessing. To the question of the merchant as to who he was, Vladyka answered, "You will see me in the Chudov Monastery in Moscow." With this, the Metropolitan became invisible.

The merchant's road home passed through Moscow, where he spent a few days. While in the Kremlin, he visited the Chudov Monastery, where at that time His Eminence, Metropolitan Philaret of Moscow, was celebrating the Divine Liturgy. The merchant was greatly amazed when he recognized him to be his rescuer, since it came true that he saw him in the Chudov Monastery! At the end of the service he immediately went to the Holy Trinity Metochion, personally told Vladyka everything that had happened, and with tears expressed his gratitude. Having listened, Vladyka gave him a small icon of St. Alexis as a blessing and strictly forbade him to talk about what had happened, but to attribute what had happened not to Vladika himself, but to St. Alexis.

(26)

On the road to Moscow, a peasant stopped at a house to rest and, since it was already evening, and it was snowing heavily, he was invited to spend the night. However, hoping to reach Moscow, which was only a few versts away, he again set out on the road. Having gone three versts from the house, he lost his way because of the terrible blizzard. He collapsed from exhaustion and was extremely afraid of freezing to death. He then saw a shadow approaching him, and thinking that it was some sort of beast wanting to tear him apart, he began to pray to God for forgiveness of his sins and to call upon all the saints for help. When the shadow grew closer, he saw that it was a short elder in a black riassa and hat who asked him who he was and from where. And when the peasant explained everything to him in detail, the elder took him by the hand and said, "Why have you given up? Get up, and I will lead you to the village." Feeling that his strength had returned, the peasant got up, and the two of them easily reached the village. Arriving at the dwelling, the elder said, "Stay here, the Lord be with you. Now you are out of danger." With tears of gratitude the peasant fell on his knees and asked for whom he should pray. The elder said, "Pray for Philaret of Moscow," and with these words, he became invisible.

Having spent the night in the village, the next day the peasant arrived in Moscow and went about to various monasteries trying to find his savior, and although he found monks by that name, he did not recognize them as the one who had helped him. Having spent a few days in Moscow and not satisfying his desire, he was already preparing for his return trip. Going through the Nikolsky gates, he met an unknown merchant, who, noticing his sad countenance, and assuming that he was needy, wanted to give him alms. The peasant would not take the alms, and when asked the reason for his sorrow, he related what had happened. Having heard his story, the unknown man said, "Probably our Metropolitan saved you," after which he gave him directions to the Holy Trinity Metochion. He immediately set out, and he arrived there just as Vladyka, returning from the Synodal office was stepping out of his carriage. The peasant recognized him right away, and falling on his knees, he exclaimed, "There is my savior!" Vladyka ordered him to be quiet and to follow him to his chambers, where the peasant explained everything to him in detail. Having listened to him, Vladyka said, "Do not attribute this to me, but pray to St. Sergius - he is the one who saved you." Then Vladyka gave him a small icon of St. Sergius.

(27)

A. had the custom of reading the Psalter, but one time she somehow forgot her rule and did not fulfill it for a few days. Soon she had in a dream in which she saw that Vladyka was celebrating the Divine Liturgy in the church of the Holy Trinity Metochion, after which he began to bless the people. When A. approached to receive his blessing, Vladyka asked her, "Are you reading the Psalter of David?" Being ashamed to tell the truth in front of all the people, she answered that she was reading it, but Vladyka responded, "Completely?" Surprised by Vladyka's clairvoyance, she admitted that for a few days she had not completed her rule. Then Vladyka said, "Without fail, you must read it every day," after which she woke up.

(28)

Once, M. N. found a job as a clerk for the director of an accounting firm. The director was of the Lutheran faith, however, and for M. N., raised in piety and the fear of God, it was very difficult to break the fast. Therefore throughout the course of two fasting periods, she ate only tea and bread. But since those who worked with her began to make comments concerning this before the beginning of the Nativity Fast, she decided to eat meat. The next night she had a dream and saw that Vladyka was riding in his carriage very slowly across Red Square to the Saviour gate and was blessing the multitudes of people who were crowded around him. M. N. had already lost hope of receiving his blessing when suddenly Vladyka turned to her and asked sternly "What do you need?" She answered, "To receive your blessing." Vladyka said to her, "You know how strictly you must keep the fast, for the Apostles fasted, even the Saviour Himself fasted!"

At this point she awoke and firmly decided to keep the fasts. After a year she saw Vladyka in a dream for a second time, and he was celebrating the Divine Liturgy. At the end he began to bless all the people, but when M. N. approached him he said, "Wait." He returned to the altar, brought out an icon, and blessed her with it saying, "This is for you as a blessing, for the Lord loves those who keep the fasts." After this she awoke, and after that she always strictly kept all the fasts.

(29)

In a noble family, a brother and sister differed in their opinion concerning Vladyka Philaret: The woman respected him very much, while her brother allowed himself to speak about him disrespectfully. Once they had a conversation concerning Vladyka's clairvoyance. The brother not only did not believe it, but also even planned to put Vladyka to the test by deceit, and in spite of his sister imploring him to abandon his plan, he remained unmoved. Dressing up in very old clothes, he set out for the Holy Trinity Metochion. When Vladyka stepped outside, the brother told him that he had experienced a great misfortune: his estate had burned down, and now he was destitute. Hearing this, Vladyka returned to his quarters and then brought a package containing money which he then gave to him with these words: "Here, this is for you for your possessions that burned." When he returned home, he showed his sister the money, which he had received from Vladyka, and with delight he recounted everything in detail, all of which was very grievous to her. On the following day he received news that on the very hour when he was with Vladyka, a fire at his estate had burned possessions of his worth exactly the amount he had received from the Metropolitan. This coincidence astounded him greatly, and he immediately went to Vladyka, sincerely told him about everything, and with tears asked his forgiveness. After this he firmly believed in the clairvoyance of Vladyka, and greatly respected him.

(30)

There was once a woman who for a long time lived in the most pitiful and difficult conditions, and finally began to fall into despair. One evening, after many tears, she fell asleep and saw Vladyka, who entered with a censer in his hand, censed her entire room, and then approached her and censed her three times. Upon awakening, she felt an unusual lightness in her soul, and from that day on was completely at peace.